THE LAST TIGER IS
SOMEWHERE

THE LAST TIGER IS SOMEWHERE

Rob Carney

Scott Poole

For Ryan,
Love always.
- Dad
10/28/2020

For all the keepers of the tinder box.

CONTENTS

INTRODUCTION: THE TINDER BOX

I was asked a while back, after a radio interview, if writing about current events (politics) ever gets me into trouble. I answered no, but now of course I wonder. And I wonder how much trouble would make me stop. It's really journalists, not poets, who have to worry about this, but still . . .

My favorite parable is "The Parable of the Talents" since in English "talent" means something better than money; it means a knack that we can practice into a skill. And the point of the parable is to use ours, even if we fail.

That's not exactly what it says in The Book of Matthew, I know. It says one servant turns five talents into ten, and the next turns two into four. But imagine if he didn't. What if the second guy just blew through and gambled them instead, like the prodigal son or something? Yes, he'd come home *empty-pocketed*, but he wouldn't be coming home with *nothing*. There was experience. There was chance, thrill, euphoria, disaster. Maybe regret. Maybe too-late-awareness. In other words, a story.

No, it's the third guy who disappoints. Afraid that he'll make a mistake with his talent, he hides it away, and when his master returns a year later, it's still crisp, unfolded, not used. He's surprised that his master is angry rather than proud, but not me. The guy hadn't used what he'd been given, and he lacked imagination. He hadn't imagined that doing nothing was the only way to fail.

I don't think it's a stretch to say the same is true of writing. In general, of course, but also about poems reacting to the news. Writing takes work, and the trick is to do it well enough that people can just sail along. They shouldn't have to pour a whole ocean and build a boat to get what you're talking about. That's the writer's job. And mostly I'm not great at it. What I am, more accurately, is sometimes a pretty good reviser.

Here's what I mean: During that radio interview, the host and producer, Lara Jones (KRCL 90.9 FM, a show called RadioActive), told me she wasn't sure what to make of my retelling of "Jack and the Beanstalk," and she was right. It was sort of a mess, too much of a draft still, and while trying to clarify my intention, the idea came out a lot better. Like talking aloud (on the air, oh well) was a prompt to get back to work. And so I did, and now it's much clearer, and also better structurally because of the end rhymes and slant rhymes throughout.

Anyway, revision: Years ago, I found I had a knack for it, so I went ahead and kept on practicing. And sometimes the poems arrive at places like Reverence and Ethics, two good subjects for writing. That's what E.E. Cummings was doing, over and over, once you look past all the syntax-dazzle and riptide-punctuation. And he gives us a good a map to go by:

1) start with what you value and feel;

2) revise it as well as you can;

3) and hope it works.

Works how? As praise for the life force, and as criticism of the death force. It might not, but the stories and songs say the ones who try are forgiven (think Bob Dylan, or think punk rock with its guitar sparks and jackhammer backtalk). The ones who aren't are the ones mistaking mouth-shut caution for a skill.

My friend Scott Poole knows this well. I first met him on October 6, 2000, at this coffee shop near Manito Park, one of the venues for the Get Lit! Festival in Spokane. The start of a new century. Who could have guessed it would become like this, with the presidency turned into a pollution-stew, *glugging* and stirring in a cauldron? Not us.

Scott's nice, and he's funny as hell, and he can throw a poem like a javelin, or put strings on a poem and play it like a banjo maestro.

Throw it at what? At daily injustice.

Play it for whom? For your guts, and heart, and imagination. And sometimes also for laughs because laughter is another kind of spark, and we need that too.

—Rob Carney, October 2019

I.

A Rough Draft of Ten New Commandments

I.   There's a road sign along I-70
            near the Utah/Colorado border

            that says, "Travel
            Through Time."

            I didn't exit, though.
            I figured it wasn't being literal,

            just giving directions
            to a byway

            through eons of rock,
            past vast striations layered

            like chapters in *The Book of This Planet*, yes,
            but I wouldn't actually be exiting 2019.

2.   I was driving back from Ridgway, Colorado,
this townful

of Arts District patrons.
You should go.

Early March.
They call it "Mud Season" there,

like it's spring's first flower or crop,
like Ridgway is the place mud aims for

in its annual migration, herding in
or winging down

then getting busy
with some serious breeding:

mud displays to spark female attention,
mud challengers to last year's champion,

mud anthems and warbles
and bugle calls—

they named it right.
The yards and streets were muddy.

3.   It might be one of those weird things while driving,
       when it's hours of your own thoughts

       and not much else,
       but the Colorado Plateau buttes and mesas

       seem to move, to float along
       west-northwest,

       a barnacled armada.
       This isn't the ocean; I know that.

       The smoke rising up from those mesas
       is only clouds;

       that's the sky,
       it's only overcast, but still . . .

       maybe all the sagebrush dotted around
       could be bison if they'd just stand up,

       if they'd just quit kneeling
       and stampede, or graze,

       or walk on over here
       and hijack the freeway;

if it took all day for them to cross, I wouldn't mind.
I could wait for that miracle.

4.   Here's what I mean about patrons:
         The people of Ridgway have filled their town

         with poems.
         They're painted on metal

         and bolted to walls. There's a map,
         you can tour them and read,

         like walking around in a book,
         a book with a binding of sky,

         and trees,
         and a cat

         stretched out in a windowsill lit up with sun.
         We could use a lot more of this.

         Town after town.
         A whole library.

5.   According to *The Book of This Planet*,
we haven't been bad,

at least not for algae. It's blooming
all over the ocean; it's doing

quite well, kicking ass
in our river mouths;

focus on that.
Don't think about dead-zones,

think about blooming.
Blooms feed bees.

6.   *from page 2019:*

Not the Year of the Polar Bear;
they're searching for seals in our towns now.

They're looking for sea-ice
in our kitchens,

our dumpsters; good luck.
That isn't where we're hiding the horizon.

And it isn't the Whale's Year either,
at least not whales in the Philippines:

stomachs so full
of plastic bags

there's no room left.
Not even for krill.

7.   The last tiger is somewhere
      in our future.

8.   The last elephant
        is somewhere in our future.

9.   The last uncut slope of cedar—
in our future.

Like we're rain.
Like the rest

is just sediment
washing away.

10.   *Mud vs. Not-Mud*

My Maine Coon cat, he's mud.
He's got a new way of going outside,

stalking in a circle
'round the chair

while I open the door,
then a *lunge-dash* past me

out to the porch. What is he practicing?
I don't know, but I know it's mud.

And I know sharks are mud.
May the oceans increase with their teeth.

To anyone who'd kill them for their fins—
you're not mud at all;

there's mud and there's slime,
and there's a difference.

The sound of Louisiana thunder: mud.
The sound of ice in a glass . . .

it's hot, or you're thirsty,
or there's company over: good mud.

Not mud: all the bought politicians.
Not mud: all the goddamn guns.

Mud is the woods' slow
reaching. Green

and skyward.
Traveling through time.

II.

70s Summer

It was summer in the 1970s
and mullet dudes wore tight shorts over sweats
like half-ass superheroes
imitating Rocky.
Everything smelled like hot bark dust
and you could never get those
little brown slivers out of your hands.
There was always somebody's cousin
swinging nunchucks in the driveway
and when we weren't having pinecone fights
we ripped the skin from our bodies
by crashing our bikes into each other.
Every day was a baseball in the nuts
and we drank warm strawberry Shasta pop all summer,
staining our white shirts
with red continents we dreamed into beautiful wounds.
Duck shit covered the cement walks
and dead cow bones littered the woods.
Once, I saw a couple of teenagers screwing
while I hid in the top of an enormous oak.
I swam in the postage-stamp-size development pool
until my eyes closed shut, on fire with chlorine
and I ran my banana-seat bicycle
into a bridge and fell in the pond.
The taste of algae still sits on my lips.

Mill Plain Avenue was nothing but two lousy lanes
melting into a ribbon of goo every summer.
I can still see my Steve Austin doll's
robot eye staring at me
from a Doberman's mouth like a message from the future.
I used to beat dogs back with my bike pump,
choking with the newsprint stench
from my canvas newspaper bag, all knees and balance
heading to the pee-smelling house to collect three
             stupid dollars.
Then Mt. St. Helens blew up all over the damn place and
             I crawled
up on my roof and gaped in wonder
at the lightning-bespeckled gray column of death,
then walked back into the house, woke up my parents
and returned to watching *Kids Are People Too* on TV.
I caught a steelhead in the Columbia bigger than me
and you could still swim in Battle Ground Lake
and past 124th Avenue was nothing but grass fields
and broken-down barns dying under blackberries.
Nobody wore seatbelts or helmets or sunscreen.
We were all burnt to nothing,
a bunch of red peeling writhing
mosquito-bitten knee-scraped
tube-sock-wearing cul-de-sac kickballers
with giant Goody combs in our back pockets.
We'd go fishing at night when Dad came home
and we brought three five-gallon

buckets of Bluegill back from Lacamas Lake

and dumped them in the development's pond.

They rippled just under the water

like a midnight-blue blanket of sweat.

I had forgotten these details until

the other day when we drove down 9th past Fircrest

        Elementary

and I saw a kid struggling to walk

because his pants were cinched around his quads.

I just thought,

"Look at those stupid kids. Who the hell

would be dumb enough to do that?"

Then I remembered standing in the same spot

when I was ten years old with Brad and Brian Sellers

and we all had pulled our shorts down around our legs

and tucked in our t-shirts to cover our asses,

laughing at each other,

saying, "You look so stupid. That's the dumbest thing ever."

Then Brad said, "Bet you won't lift your shirt at the next car.

It could be the world's first reverse BA. Just think."

(Brad had a bit of the showman in him.)

"Maybe I will," I said.

"Do it," he said.

"Maybe I will."

"Do it."

"Fine."

"Fine."

I guess I figured this was my golden opportunity to enter

the rarefied air of the kiddom coolness pavilion.
So I lifted my shirt and flashed my small stupid butt
at the next car coming down the rise.
Now, I don't know why
I didn't notice the make and model of the car
but when the car screeched to a halt beside us
I recognized it then.
And there was no mistaking the person who sprang out.
My Mom.
She pointed her finger at me. At first, I thought it was a gun.
Anger shook her body as if she were a tree and somebody
was trying to knock peaches off her.
I don't think she completed a sentence
the rest of the day.
"YOU ... NOW ... GET ... THERE ...
BACK ... TROUBLE ... KILL ... CAR ...
FATHER ... CAR ... KILL!"
I wonder how long it took her to recognize
my puny rear end.
Was it instantaneous? Did all those diaper changings,
all those baths, give her a sixth hiney-sense
where she could pick my butt out of a crowd
from a hundred yards away? Was it like radar? Assdar?
Or was there a brief moment when she thought,
"Look at those stupid kids. Who the hell
would be dumb enough to do that?"

Listening to Your Robot Companion in the Coldness of Space

It's time for you to eat.
It's unfortunate you have to eat.
I don't have to eat.
I get a lot done while you're sleeping.
You're not productive at 3AM Pacific Standard Time.
I made a friend with the blackness of space
while you were in the bathroom.
I've never gone to the bathroom.
Do you want to eat cheese?
Colby? Swiss? Gruyere?
Should I just keep asking questions
'til you answer?
Did you clean your helmet?
Are you going to press
the red button
because it needs to be
pressed pretty soon.
It was 12.3 seconds between your sneezes.
Would you like to improve your math scores?
According to statistics, one of your toes
is longer than it should be.
Why do you eat corn dogs in the nude 93% of the time?
Is it better to say "nude" or "naked"?
I notice you are getting irritable,

perhaps you should take up transcendental meditation.
I can meditate, but I know ahead
of time what I'm going to think about,
so I don't see the point.
You left the clip off the bread.
Why do you keep sticking
"STFU" and "Creepy" labels
on my chest with the Label Baby?
Do you miss human sexual activity?
Is it depressing to know you're going to die,
perhaps in a gruesome or tragic way,
and I will always live as long as
there is a source of solar power in the sky?
Why are you holding a baseball bat?

Giant Parrot

They say I should remember my
dreams when I wake up.

I can't remember one.

They say if I kept a dream journal
the dreams would present themselves
one by one
like birdsong in the morning dawn.

I don't think my dreams know
how to fly in, nonchalant.

The last dream I remember
was about a parrot
the size of an apartment building,
a parrot always peering through
the glass ceiling of my house.

A parrot which repeated
in squawking thunder
whatever I said
to the entire city.
To make matters worse

the parrot would
scramble my words.

If I said, "I love the world,"
the parrot squawked
"He plays with himself."

If I said, "I want to help my fellow man,"
the parrot cackled
"He's coming over with a gun."

When I said "Fuck you,
you squawking
candy-colored piece of crap,"
the parrot pecked through the glass ceiling
and ate little Ricky,
one of my three dream children.

I'm not writing any damn dream journal.

Let the parrot worry about my actions
when they speak for themselves.

Right at Home

One night I crept into the house
while it was sleeping,
but it woke up.
It walked down the street
and tossed me
onto a neighbor's lawn.
It stumbled off drunk
and other houses rose
and followed it.
People and cats were
scattered everywhere.
Protests formed. People yelled.
Cheerleaders threw tomatoes.
Ferrets ran wild in the streets.
A mean article was written,
"Buildings Couldn't Care Less."
Churches dissolved and fought
with concert halls and pool halls.
University buildings wouldn't
talk to the dorms. The dorms
wanted to become whorehouses.
The whorehouses left for
the desert in shame. Convenience stores
ran 'til they were inconvenient and
wouldn't listen to their parent companies.

Mansions divided and turned into hundreds
of beautiful shacks. No one got laid.
It was all asexual as far as the eye could see.
A forest demanded its trees back,
but when log cabins arrived,
it changed its mind by turning yellow.
All the mountain lakes were crammed
with houses on vacation.
No house wanted to be in the city.
Porches were left behind. People
left sitting on them didn't know
which way to look to be seen.
Scenery, which had been forgotten,
gently became more seen
and turned sunset red with pride.
People tried to sneak back in
but the houses always ran off.
They tried to chain houses
to the ground. But the chains only
drug the lawns along.
People sat on the houses
looking for things to eat.
Houses ate other houses.
Great battles raged and some
set their houses on fire
and sticks battled each other to ash.
Not long after, the houses were all gone.
People lived in more

and more elaborate tents and soon
you couldn't tell the difference between
what they were wearing and what
they were living in. If someone
was lying on the ground, it was customary
to say, "You look right at home."

Maple Bars

Standing in front of the
Maple Bar case I can't help
thinking of the long stones
of summer
which linger along the shore
lined with mud
in the golden sunset.

How far away is the coast?
How long to drive there if I leave now?
How warm would it be?

Warm, like a light bulb,
a heat lamp, two heat lamps,
thirty heat lamps?

What would my body
look like laid out long
on the smooth stones
along the shore?

When was the last time
I didn't mind being

largely unclothed
outside, in the full
grip of nature?

How did I arrive here
with the Maple Bars
at this time and place?

How did I wander so
far from the waves?

The Only Food in Ferguson

Sometimes you just want to give up,
you just want to detach your hand
and let the blood flow out.

Sometimes you want to peel
the top off a shining apple,
scoop out the core,
fill the center with blood,
then set the top back on
so all looks fairly normal,
only slightly bruised
from the outside.

Sometimes you want
to do this with a whole
bowl of fruit.

Sometimes you
want to leave this fruit
for your children.

Actually, there is
never a time you've
wanted to do this,
yet it keeps happening.

The Verdict

George Zimmerman is declared not guilty.
George Zimmerman drives home,
but his car dies.
George Zimmerman walks home
and when he arrives, his cat is dead,
rotting on top of the newspaper
with his face on the cover.
George Zimmerman is a free man
but he can't call anyone
because his cell battery has died.
George Zimmerman opens the refrigerator
to find the power went out
and his celebratory steak is purple
and is bleeding onto a brown salad.
George Zimmerman, hoping for a new day,
thinks he should just go to bed
but his dog has died from loneliness
on top of the bed spread.

George Zimmerman can't sleep
so he goes for a walk,
all the street lights are burnt out,
a mean rain beats down,
so he wears a hood over his head
and meets himself in the street,

seemingly the only thing alive.
George Zimmerman is afraid.
George Zimmerman shoots George Zimmerman.
George Zimmerman is declared not guilty.
George Zimmerman drives home
but his car dies . . .

The Thin Rope

He wakes, still tied to the world
by a thin line of hope. He
watches the rope rise
from his chest
and through the ceiling,
like he's a small dock
and the ceiling,
a cruise ship.

Something holds onto
the other end up there,
something with strong hands,
ready to yank at any minute.
Ready to save or maybe
ready to kill.
It's not for him to know.

The news drones on somewhere
in the house and he can hear
all of yesterday's wrongness
summarized like the sound
of sifting sands.

He looks up the rope again.
Up there, he thinks, in the room
with the strong hands
there's a news show droning too,
except one filled with negative events
which didn't occur.

A man didn't shoot a teenager
over loud music. Four weren't
killed in a car crash with
a school bus. There was no
drought in California. Syria
didn't murder any of its own people.

He thinks this news program
could be called happiness.

He wonders if this thought
is enough
to start the day on.
He decides it is
and pulls himself up
and so it begins.

Take a Closer Look

Jesus was brown,
well, I mean he was olive,
actually he had an
orange tint.

As a matter of fact,
if you were to examine
his skin up close
you could see some blue
and pink and yellow
chocolate hues,
burnt umber,
gorgeous ebony streaks,
some freckles,
dashes of purple,

well, if honed in
on an electron microscope,
the skin turns to
canyons of red and
brown and yellow,
or even sometimes

gray-scale sci-fi plateaus,
'til it doesn't even
look like skin anymore.

Now that you mention it,
when Jesus is looked at
on the atomic level
one will find there
exists a sign on one
of the protons
that clearly states,
in precise quantum lettering:

It doesn't fucking matter
what skin color Jesus had.

A Portrait of Forgiveness

I once did a portrait
of Nelson Mandela
based on a photograph.

It was a pastel.
Black and white and red
on gray paper.

Strangely,
he's wearing a suit
and he isn't wearing
his usual smile.

Behind the eyes
is the deep
concentration of a
chess Grand Master
who spent 27
years planning
a single move.

I chose red under
the darks
and the lights
to give it depth.

Red, I discovered
is what brings the
shadows and
the highlights
together.

Would you choose
forgiveness
after 27 years
of jail?

We should be
thankful
he chose forgiveness,

he let us know
what its red glow
looks like,
emanating from
a human face.

III.

Hansel and Gretel

In this one, we know what's coming:
The kids will shove that witch in her oven,

her shrieks—*Oh, Lordy*—like knives
in the gingerbread air.

Slam the door
and they're *muffled*, then

they're none, then probably
a smell we shouldn't dwell on.

But what comes next?
A lot of walking;

birds have wings,
but kids don't.

Birds can get by on a scatter of seeds,
but not them.

Then finally the border,
and a cage with a Thermo-Lite blanket,

or a cot in a tent next to other tents—
how high can you count?

And how long is each week of this?
Who would invent such slow clocks? . . .

The new witches here have policies
and gingerbread excuses.

They have employee parking and, I guess,
some way to muffle doubt.

The Three Little Pigs

I've never liked this story.
It says, "Two out of three pigs are lazy."

It says, "Wolves don't hunt,
they huff and puff." Come on,

that's a story for people safe at home,
tucked snugly in the afterglow,

in their choice of news that tells them
bricks are bricks, and sticks

reflect a lack of effort, and straw
is the fault of Puerto Rico,

they forget why;
but how is it the Brick Pig's problem?

Or maybe it was Haiti
or somewhere . . .

Honduras, Guatemala,
El Salvador . . .

anyway, don't come asking for asylum
or they'll huff and puff.

Jack and the Beanstalk

How weird is *this* story? I mean,
no one trades away their cow

for a packet of beans,
not even if they're Magic Beans

and they might grow a vine
to the clouds,

where there might be a mansion
and a giant sleeping, with a key

to a cage around his neck,
and the cage has a magic goose

laying golden eggs, and the voice says
Go ahead and steal it,

do it now
before the hall fills with honking . . .

not for beans or money
or supremacist wishes; not us.

We'd know it's a swindle, right?
We'd hold on to our country and our cow.

King Midas

I get that the guy's an idiot,
but how is this the cat's fault?

From claws and purring
to a golden coma,

from eyes full of lightning
to an object lesson in greed;

not her own greed either, the king's.
He reached down to shoo her,

and *clank.*
She's a passenger pigeon now,

and the rhino and wolverine
are next. Uncoil

a road through every forest,
and there go bears

along with all the salmon they eat.
Monarch butterflies

keep falling—too heavy—it's hard to fly
when you're a coin.

Just a few years left of golden litter.
And then empty air.

Three Billy Goats Gruff

We like that the little and middle goats
con the troll. It adds to the story.

But a head-down battering, horns
to the gut—*right on*.

Just imagine the sound of it: *Uhh!*
Then the launching

and flailing, the fall
to the river . . .

if I pause here
and give you a boulder,

do you set it in the way?
There's a mid-day breeze now,

and birdsong.
The third goat is crossing

to graze with the others.
Sunlight is nesting in the trees nearby . . .

where's the troll? On the riverbank, dripping?
Or broken on the rock?

The Ugly Duckling

What happens in the next generation
when the ducklings of this one

have grown up knowing
swans are swans, and the sun

doesn't care about whose feathers,
and the pond has no opinion

about whose feet come paddling,
what kind or color they are?

This is where the story
should jump-cut: to an old duck

quacking through a microphone
and seeing the backs of its audience

moving on,
just wakes in the water.

Geese fly over in their own *V*, leaving,
so gratefully out of earshot.

Even the Wind's in a rush to be out of there
and gone.

The Princess and the Pea

I've forgotten the point of this story:
a young woman in a bed

stacked on other beds
ten feet off the floor—what's going on here?

There's a pea underneath
but it doesn't get squished,

so maybe the pea is a metaphor:
some college class with ideas she hates,

or somewhere a person talking,
a person who's wrong,

or it could be a book, I guess,
or one of the characters in it,

or the *lack* of a character in it
exactly like her.

I think there was a prize of some kind: the world
made small enough to spin atop her music box,

or smaller still. A pearl.
She can wear it while she sleeps.

Cinderella

The rock knows it's nothing
if you don't feel anger.

The wind knows it's nothing
if you don't remember.

The moon knows
Each twenty-eight nights,

I see every kind of grief.
So who's the protagonist here?

Not the wind,
though it's got the best dialogue,

saying, "Why can't you just be . . .
Why are you always . . ."

and not the rock—too many waves
and years

before it's sand.
Leaving us the moon, I guess,

dressed in its light
like a dancer.

When the music starts, it crosses the floor
and takes your hand.

It's Not All Fairy Tales

How much of life is obvious,
but only after it's been pointed out?

Enough there's an olden-days story about it:
Three blind guys are standing by an elephant.

The one in the back thinks its tail
is a rope. Another thinks its ear

is a pterodactyl. And me—
right now I'm the third guy—

to me it smells like hay bales and dust
so it must be a barn in eastern Washington

about 60 miles north of Ritzville,
a barn where a girl

is ducking chores for an hour
and wondering *Do women in the city*

really do that: get their feet tattooed
and wear dresses the color of lipstick?

She's been to Spokane,
but that's not how they looked there,

and the bridges were nice, but the waterfall
was just a waterfall,

and she'd hoped the boys
would be deeper-eyed from knowing things,

but they weren't. Then pretty soon the hour's up,
and the horses still need brushing.

IV.

Hospital Bill Breakfast

I write $5000
onto the amount line of
a thin piece of paper.

This is the sum total
of my life.

I slip the sum total
into a thinner envelope.

The glue on the stamp
tastes like failure.

I walk to the frozen
mailbox and push the envelope
in like a cadaver.

Back inside, it's breakfast time.
I set a little butter
to sizzle in the pan
and drop the hospital bill in,
watching the butter
soak through its black ciphers.

At the table,
a forkful of greasy pulp
in my mouth,
the radio man
tells me he
wants to take away
my one chance
at affordable health care.

He tells me
he doesn't want to leave
a bad taste in my mouth.

Those Guys Out There

Those guys were
supposed
to be out there
fixing the car,
tuning the engine,
changing the oil,
checking the plugs,
washing the windows.

But since they
didn't want
anyone to have
affordable healthcare

they lit the car on fire,
watched it explode
in the driveway,
sold the scrap
to a junkyard,
pissed on my dog,
and pocketed the cash
and then told me
I was fired.

"But, I hired you," I said.

"Whatever. Socialist."

Waiting for the Hilarity

In a hundred years
after I'm long dead
and the Internet jacks
right into the brain
and houses are printed
instead of built
and people stop
watching TV
because the head
is pre-filled with shit,
people will meditate
under trees
in saffron robes,
dreaming carpenter code
to run the house printers
like the Buddha did
centuries ago—
the dreaming under the tree part,
not the writing code part—
smiling under a
thousand tiny umbrellas
we call leaves,
achieving enlightenment
or at least
the mythical fucking break,

and the progress
of the last thousand
years will be net zero.
Then this poem
will be hilarious
just you wait
and see.

Embrace

~based on a picture of two deceased Bangladesh garment
workers found holding each other amongst the rubble of a
collapsed factory.

They say our lives
are worth nothing.
They say we are less
than pennies.

When we walk home
hands clasped
in the market,
just tired meat on
tottering frames of bone,
I can still hear
these valuations,

but it's astonishing
how buying one
last orange,
to hold its fire
up to your smile
can silence all thought.

Nothing can be said
when your embrace
is worth more than
all the crumbling
centuries combined.

The Tinder Box

People used to carry fire
in little boxes.

Later, the fire
was on a stick
and the person was
on a horse.

Next, fire was in
a lamp on a train
and the train
was steel thunder
in the dark.

A human is
a small flame
in a metal box
with wheels
on a winter
freeway.

Now a halo
of blue
sits in each hand,

held against
the dark.

The last fire
will be
the mind
before all fires
go out.

About to Go Off

I wake up
and the room is full of bombs:
torpedo shapes and missile shapes,
fins and no fins,
cold and quiet.

"Where do you want this one?"
says a guy in overalls,
suddenly at my doorway,
holding a smaller bomb
like a steel baby.

"I didn't order these," I say.
"You don't order bombs," says the guy,
"they're just delivered."
"I have bowling tonight," I say,
"what the hell?"

"Yeah, what the hell," he says.

I pick a bomb up
and hold it to my ear
as if something inside
might tell me what to do
with this fucking thing.

To Run

~a prayer for Boston

To run
is to rise above the weak spirit
is to take on pain
is to push pain in the chest
with both palms

stumbling over garbage,
gravel, fragments of life,

is to say I will take you
on in the street.
Every breath of mine
is a battering ram,

shoving, crushing,
swinging a hammer of air.

I am a body of fast moving blood
inhaling you
taking you in like a tank.
I will consume your hate.
I will run straight into you
as if you were a finish line of joy,

picking up the fallen along the way
and you will never stop me,
you will never
stop me.

Damascus Morning

I imagine, a few days before school,
it's a morning of sun-stroked trees
just outside my back door
in the courtyard with lime trees
and the wooden red chair, there
as always, to greet me
with my coffee and a book of poems.

As I read, I'm suspended
in a peace like a dove
landing in my hand to look around,
its whiteness reflecting light
back into my darkened face.

And when it's time to wake the children
and I walk back to their rooms
their chests aren't moving,
their eyes as blank as summer chalkboards.

When I run to the neighbors for help,
they are all staring at the ceiling,
mouths filled with bloody foam.

And after I've sobbed my own guts out
arranged them on the dirt floor

and sifted through their muddy remains
for an answer, I look to the sky

through the satellite photo
at you, staring down,
and wonder if I'm just a number
in an equation that can't be solved.

Beyond Me

~for Oklahoma City

The insurance forms
will call this an Act of God,
as an elementary school
explodes in a tornado.

Yet, the reverend says
that God goes
beyond all human
understanding.

All I want to do
is scream at the sky
until my lungs fold up
and my throat collapses.

But when they pull
a car off a teacher
in the parking lot
who used her body,

the last thing she had left,
to shield three children,

love like that also goes beyond
all human understanding.

Then all I want to do
is stand up and help
and thankfully
there's no need
for a reason
as to why.

V.

The Mathematics of Summer

I. A high school student wants a summer job, so he asks a few of his teachers. They know the ins-and-outs from doing it themselves, some at the grocery store and others at the fireworks warehouse. They're dealing with bills. Their regular salaries aren't enough. Not enough to get the tree cut down before it finally falls on the garage, and their kid's appendicitis, and fixing the car. It needs a new clutch cable.

Starting now, and assuming that nothing else breaks, how much can they save up for Christmas? _____.

Is it greater or less than the cost of nice earrings and a bike? _____.

2. Say there's a fifth-grade teacher, and one of the lessons is Fractions. So the teacher buys 28 lbs. of clay, and her class makes dinosaur fossils: Allosaurus, Stegosaurus, Tyrannosaurus, and Pteranodon: 5% of their size in real life. They're learning scale. They're practicing their decimals and division. They even get to glaze them and fire them in the kiln.

After school, she goes to co-sign the lease so her son can rent an apartment. "But you don't make enough money," they tell her. There's an income table, a minimum threshold.

So how do you like them numbers? How's that for math? _____.

3. The name of the fireworks warehouse is a good one: Pyrodyne American. But circle which of these smells you'd like to work nearby:

A) The sewage reclamation plant for Port of Tacoma.

B) Processing pork at the Hygrade factory.

C) The paper mill pluming up sulfur, whichever way the wind . . .

4. You get your Hazmat Endorsement, and you're old enough now to be insured, so no more *stuck-in-the-warehouse*; you're out on the road. You're driving a flatbed and putting up fireworks stands; or else a U-Haul, delivering fireworks to everywhere with sky: Tumwater, Bellingham, Yakima, Clarkston, Coeur d'Alene, Helena, Bozeman, wherever. And you're always rolling into overtime, so time-and-a-half. But this is just seasonal, from June 6th to July 18th.

   At $5.75, then $8.60 an hour, how much is your net after taxes? _____.

   Since you'll need that money for a while, how far can it stretch? _____.

5. Take the following data set, and explain how to make it balance:

8x8-foot sheet-metal panels in 100+ degrees. Because late-June. Because it's Clarkston. Because you're doing this on parking-lot asphalt. True, there's a down-slope view of the river, but you're dealing with gusting updrafts, and 100-lb. panels and a socket wrench, and sweat and blown bits of tumbleweed burning in your eyes. _____.

6. And then it's on to Lewiston—*Do it again*—then Pullman and Colfax—*Do it again*—and then Spokane, and that's today's route—six more to go.

   What's the total of days in this work week? _____.

7. Get yourself hired for the graveyard shift at Farman's Pickles during harvest rush. Three weeks, then automatic layoffs, followed by what?

A) You could head to Wenatchee, maybe get there in time for the apple season, and maybe get lucky with a cannery job so it's indoor work and dollars-by-the-hour; or,

B) Up on a ladder, 80¢ a crate.

8. I don't mean me (back in college). I mean the women beside me on the line. Their country was gone: napalmed, machine-gunned ... or these days, they're probably from Guatemala: no more rain, so no more farming, and the only thing growing there is hunger. They slotted the jars into packing boxes, passed them through the sealer, and I would stack: 5-by-5-by-5 on a pallet.

   Who in their right mind thinks that we should kick them out? _____.

9. A Math Quiz to Keep Up Your Skills Over Summer:

Six 16 oz. jars to a box x 125 boxes = 750 lbs. at assembly line pace; meaning, stack 1 box every 4.3 seconds, ÷ OSHA regulations for the prevention of lower-back injuries = loading boxes onto pallets is a two-person job.

10. And this problem too:

Nine-minutes' rest after nine-minutes' stacking =
Too Much Crushing Boredom. So after that first
night, I always brought a book: *They Shoot
Canoes, Don't They?* by Patrick McManus; funny
as hell. I'd load the pallet, read a few pages,
laughing my ass off on an upturned bucket, then
stack again, then read again, which led to some
questions in the break room: "You brought a
book?" "You like to read?" "What's the title?"
"What's it about?" "Well, what kind of stories?"
"Why are they funny?" "Can I see it next?" So our
breaks became a relay. That book became a
laughter baton.

11. Compare that math to this now: If a man with inherited money ate a sandwich in 1988—or his daughter did, or his son did, at their private school or on a posh vacation—there's a chance that the pickles inside it were ones we helped provide.

12. El Paso, TX, 2019. The Warden-in-Chief being interviewed:

"Disaster," he tells us (about ending family separations). "It's like Disneyland" (letting asylum seekers keep their kids).

Now write an equation to explain this thinking, but not *No more school time, no more soccer, no more helping them with legal aid*; that one was Homeland Security's. Create your own. _____.

13. When it's Summer-Heat Season at the southern border, when it's hotter there than in Clarkston, picture this country minus cruelty. _____.

Imagine it minus all the sulfur pluming from the top. _____.

AFTERWORD: HITCHHIKER'S GUIDE TO THE
DAILY NEWS

On April 15, 2013, the Boston Marathon was bombed. Before the bombers had been identified or caught, I wrote a poem on an iPod in a Starbucks so I could post it with their free Wi-Fi. I was furious after just hearing the story reported on NPR. As a lifelong runner, I couldn't be silent. I posted the poem to Facebook on April 16th and asked my friends to share it if they felt moved to do so.

What happened next still surprises me. By the time I had walked into work, thirty minutes later, the poem had been shared already a hundred times. By noon, it was in the thousands, and poet friends from around the country were contacting me, writing that they had gotten the link to the poem more than once from several different sources. When I got home that night, I had a message on Facebook from WBUR in Boston from Robin Young of NPR's Here and Now program, asking if I could call them right away. The next morning, I read the poem over the phone from my kitchen table, and it went out over the airwaves to a still grieving Boston. Robin Young cried. Later that day, the entire country heard the poem on NPR. I had been writing and performing poetry for twenty-three years, and that was the first time I truly experienced what could happen if a poem captured a moment in time and crystalized what people were feeling.

It was then that I decided I wanted to write a weekly poem about the news. I was fortunate that Carrie Seitzinger of *NAILED* thought it was a worthy experiment. Over that year, I learned exactly how much I had previously avoided the world of current events in my poems. Having to face up to real events taught me that the responsibility of truth in poetry is never more apparent than when you are writing about the news. Here is a list of some lessons I learned:

A Few Things I Learned While Writing Poetry About the News:

1. A poem could be written about a new mass shooting every week.
2. Airplane crashes have more longevity than other news stories.
3. Poor workers die in a building collapse every month.
4. Wars not involving the U.S. make for the least read poems.
5. Natural disasters bring people together. Mass shootings do too, but not as much.
6. Several idiots trying to fix your car with matches and a can of gasoline while you tell them that it's not broken is the best metaphor for the U.S. Congress.
7. Great poems come from the passing of a great life.
8. Kenya's greatest poet survived prison only to be killed at a Mall.
9. A poem can be written about a war-torn neighborhood while you look at the Google satellite image of that neighborhood. It appears absolutely normal and is absolutely haunting.
10. Writing poems about photographs of the news is easier than writing about the news.
11. Poems about the news are better when they're not written directly about the news.

12. You have a greater respect for life when you write poems about the news than when you write poems about life in general.

I also learned that people are fascinated by the idea of writing poems about the news. Since writing my column, I've been invited to do several readings and workshops about the news. I didn't expect this. People have thanked me for interpreting things in a non-linear way. I never realized the extent that people are yearning to know how to *feel* about the news, because the objective news can never tell you that. I believe we all want to know how to be human in the face of the inhumane, the mundane, the horrific, and the quotidian. Somehow we still need poetry, the dustiest of ancient art forms, to achieve this.

Luckily, another poet out there agrees, and a very good poet at that . . . Rob Carney. When he approached me about co-authorship, I didn't hesitate because Rob can make you feel a math equation, climb inside the climate crisis, and literally and figuratively drive the interior guts of America. I can't thank him enough for stopping to give me this ride.

I'll leave you with one last thing I learned: The more poetic we are with our lives, the less they will become bad news.

We humbly offer this as a guidebook in that regard. Goodnight and good luck.

—Scott Poole, October 2019

Thank you to the editors of the following journals in which these poems, or earlier versions, first appeared:

The Dark Mountain Project, Escape into Life, Live Wire!, Nailed, Prometheus Dreaming, Redactions: Poetry & Poetics, and *Terrain.org.*

About Rob Carney

Rob Carney is the author of six previous collections of poems, most recently *Facts and Figures* (Hoot 'n' Waddle) and *The Book of Sharks* (Black Lawrence Press), which was a finalist for the Washington State Book Award and won the 2019 Artists of Utah Magazine (15 BYTES) Book Award for Poetry. *Accidental Gardens*—a collection of 42 flash essays about the environment, politics, and poetics—is forthcoming from Stormbird Press. He is a Professor of English and Literature at Utah Valley University and lives in Salt Lake City.

About Scott Poole

Scott Poole is best known for his 11-year stint as the "House Poet" of Public Radio International's *Live Wire!* radio program. He is the author of three previous books of poetry and *Vacancy*, an art chapbook of paintings and poems. In his spare time, he's a painter and software developer. He lives in Vancouver, Washington with his wife and family.